Plumstead Pram Pushers

Katie Beswick

Published By

Red Ogre Review & Liquid Raven Media

Authored By

Katie Beswick

Cover Artwork By

Jamie Wheeler

First Publication

2024: Los Angeles, California

ISBN

9798323309795

Library of Congress Control Number

2024938461

For Coral

Table of Contents

Foreword	1
Sonnet for a Real Slag	3
Classy Birds	4
Eating Lunch on Lamma Island	5
Slaggy Manor	6
Jackie Loses Her Virginity	7
Morning Song	8
Pike	9
52A	10
Dream Lover	11
After School Round Jackie's Nan's	12
Sket	13
Crazy	14
Yattie	15
The Blues	16
Eastenders. A Classic. 2001	17
A Sonnet for Jackie's Mother	19
A Snapshot, 1983	20
Jackie Eats Out	21
Crevasse	22
Eating In	23
Slag /noun:	24
I Imagine Looking at an Oil Painting, Which Doesn't Exist	25
Subchorionic Hematoma	26
Serving Officers	27
Hot /adjective:	28
A Thought on Valentine's Day	29
After Swimming	30
You'd Never Call	31
Dove Wing	32

Longing	35
Up the Common	36
Hungry Eyes	37
He Sees Me	38
A Haiku About Promiscuity	39
Jackie Rides the Night Bus	40
Put Your Hands Around My Neck and Tell Me You Love Me	41
Bad Sex	42
Out Loud	43
All My Fears Now Are for My Daughter: A Sestina	44
Ties	46
Slip Up Number Five	47
Jackie Visits a Launderette in New York	48
Entropy	50
A Rhyming Haiku About Class	51
Lifeblood	52
Lived Experience	53
Dispossession	54
New Year's Couplet	55
Pretty in Pink	57

Foreword

Adolescence is intense and enduring. The sensations of a newly uncanny body, along with the formative social experiences we undergo as we come of age, linger in our psyches. Trying to deal with our own desires, or lack of them, alongside budding desirability to others, feels dizzying. We are touched and touch in new ways — sometimes these touches are wanted, sometimes they are not (sometimes, it's not even clear to us what we want). Our new emotional terrain and altered body shift us to a different plane, and this shifts existing relationships. Things happen that lay the foundations for patterns played out later, with lovers and children. Our fears and joys, hopes and vulnerabilities, solidify.

    I came of age in England, in a South East London area called Plumstead, at the turn of the twenty-first century. The girls' school I attended was known locally as 'Plumstead pram pushers', in reference to the supposed sexual availability of its pupils, and the fact that a steady percentage of us had babies while still at school, or shortly after. The late 90s, after all, saw a moral panic around the figure of the teenage mother, particularly those who were perceived as working-class, as most of us were at my school. Because we were warned by teachers and television about the shame attached to young motherhood and sex in general, and maybe too because many of us had negative early sexual experiences, romantic relationships became fraught — and remained so. I and many of my friends spent years in therapy or bad relationships (or both), coming to terms with what the hell happened to us as young women, and how we could live happily in our bodies given what they'd known.

    I wrote the poems in this volume between 2014 and 2024. What started as a private way to work through complicated feelings about sex, relationships, motherhood and class became, over the years, a focused, more coherent project exploring the contours of adolescence and desire, and the patterns of intimacy we form and eventually break or settle into. I'm interested in how we see and feel ourselves, and how we are seen and felt by others — how the struggles of this form us, and how all of it is mediated by popular culture and cultures of social class. You'll see I'm also concerned with the insult slag, generally used in a British context to suggest the spoiled sexual reputation of the woman it is aimed at. Like all complex things, the slag holds fascinating contradictions — attraction and repulsion; excess and lack; shame and pleasure.

    She is in all of us, I think.

Katie Beswick
June 2024

Sonnet for a Real Slag

One day, she's gonna be obese, that slag.
Salt and vinegar McCoy's for breakfast —
pulls at your bedsheets like she's hoisting masts;
tugging pleasures, snatching at this ragbag
assortment of whatever she can blag.
Telling you half-truths no matter what you ask.
Exposing cream cake thighs, she walks past
your office window. You joke, call her a hag . . .

It's her youth what you want of her, really,
in that desperate, total way that you do.
And it's her fault, feelings you're frightened of . . .
Strength of a mother, her anger nearly
bursts through the lust.
                       Maybe you're ready to
fill up her, whole, with the shape of your love.

Classy Birds

Our screen name was ClassyBirds
and we roosted in chatrooms.
Crude wit flying out our fingertips:
sleek and shocking —
rude, like a plume of blue-tipped feathers.

Blowjobs/wankstain/illsitonyourface.

High on the power of the giggle.

    Teehee! Quod we.

We soared on the winds of our swelling sexiness.
The thick screen was a thick armour.
We perched on an office chair my dad had nicked from work;
told old men about our dirty knickers.
They kissed our virtual arses,
while our real bums — warm and pressed together —
shared the heat of an intense intimacy.
Fledgling flights for later,
our real wings shorn,
in nests we made with men false as cuckoo's eggs.

Thin screens now, in our pockets,
like terrible flat runes we carry always.
Unanswered text messages vibrate;
our flesh, hungover soft, ripples rejection.

Worms hang from our beaks,
limp and wet —
heavy with the weight of wanting.

Eating Lunch on Lamma Island

Around us, turquoise mountains rise like fish heads, surfacing open-mouthed.
My friend dips her chopsticks into roasted peanuts
and tells me she thinks our South London adolescence was a shared trauma.
We've done well to recover, she says.
We are peeling prawns, plucking pink meat from pink skins;
drinking pink wine.

I pluck a dumpling from its platter; I poke it in my open mouth.
The sea pulls away from the shore;
our boat pounds against the dock's brink.
I'm a big believer in therapy, my friend says —
She turns to our waitress, speaks in rapid scraps of Cantonese.
We're waiting for the steamed clams they forgot to bring.

My husband takes his beer and walks down to the dock.
Fishermen cast rods into the wide-open mouth of the turquoise sea.
My baby digs in the sand.
Maybe it's best, my friend says, *that we weren't the pretty girls at school.*
Light from the water dances, refracting through my wine glass.
She orders a durian mochi; we recoil from the stench.

The baby taps my leg.
In her open hand, a triangle turquoise slice, plucked from sand,
like a great slice of eye —
Some smashed tile, carrying the light weight of long history,
dappled with dark dots.
I take it from her; I close it in my fist.

I pour more pink wine;
watch my baby toddle back across the little square of beach —
mouth open in existential delight.
My friend and I discuss intellectual property law, and those pretty
girls from school, whose children are grown.
The sun moves across the turquoise water.
Our waitress brings the clams.

Slaggy Manor

Not a country estate
No
Not that
Here
Teenage girls fuck teenage boys
Or grown men
In our red uniforms
We are Plumstead Pram Pushers
Pushing half-caste babies
Single mums, smoking fags
Like slags.

Jackie Loses Her Virginity

The car park of the estate was lined with an oily, ash-coloured slush, melting slowly; it leaked into her trainers as they walked to a flat with a lacquered black door.

He was called Daniel, and he was twenty-one, with red splotches splashed across his neck. His back was lumpy with cystic acne. She stroked his lumps. Undid his shirt buttons. How to frame this as romantic, so the memory of it would not visit her later as shame, or disgust?

She switched out the lights.

His breath was sour — but then, so was hers. It was already one am, and they'd been drinking pineapple Bacardi Breezers. He had been the boyfriend of her best friend's sister, once. That was how things were. This was how things were: people told people things. It was thrilling, at the centre of all that rage.

He pushed against her, dry on dry. Then a scalding pain, and a sound like a zip, unzipping. They lay on the leather sofa. The sash window half-open — so the smell of their sour breath and the old snow, the goose flesh on her arms: all one sensation.

What she'll remember later is not the act itself so much as standing outside a betting shop the next morning, withstanding the repulsion as he kissed her — the most swirling, spiky kiss. *Lettuce in a salad spinner*, she told her friend, laughing. *A tornado of forks.*

Morning Song

                    You ordered a Turkish breakfast
                          Things blow over, you said
I nodded   Didn't tell you how when I open my mouth entire wide
  swallow you down all the spikes of my needing breaking your fall like
       branches   Lashing against your arms
          Back   Torso   Little cuts
            where those faded tattoos are
       Red slices   Lipstick kisses slashed on flesh
           where muscle moves over bone
         Veins   Your too, too human flesh
     Right where I could touch it   But I don't
I nodded   Made my blue eyes big   Full moons
             Like women in cartoons
Looked out at the flat sky   Didn't say my feelings twist up
            from a deep place   Solid
        Grown slowly   Knotted together
            Steady   Still maturing
The trunk of a tree you can hold onto and not like the leaves
                   Whimsical
                        Tumbling
Dead soon and unbothered   When the green of your eye
      Flint of it moves against the grey of mine
        Pupils expanding   Shared understanding
              I read into that
   Read into the egg yolk that pools on your plate
The air's shape between our bodies   Table-width
             The breadth of a gaze.

Pike

On the sofa at Dave's flat in Bexley Village.
Aging slowly, we down shots of whisky.
Sky outside is navy and deliciously hazy I —
I turn to him with my whole self open.
Penetrating and filled with a liquid sadness,
nestle my face against his face.
Facing each other, our lips touch with this tender authenticity.
City cynical and hardened against caring;
ring pulls from the cans we drank scattered like confetti.
Teeth against teeth —
teeth and the smooth wetness of tongues,
tonguing tenderness, like temporary passion.

On the way out the door, our friend, Alex,
explains my mistake under his breath,
breathing, *You acted so slaggy yesterday.*
Daylight and the hangover, he hands me an espresso.
So slaggy's maybe true, I think.
Think maybe that's why Dave switched so abruptly,
leaving me naked, yanking a jumper over his bare chest.
Chesty cough, he took a sip of flat beer from a green bottle.
Tells me he's off   don't even say goodbye.

52A

Stoop sitting
Weed smoking
Nights like bayonets
Wisps of indiscriminate fucking
Do you know who I am?
Mum gone Isle of Sheppey
Convalescent
Wore a belly top and thin leggings
Stripes of rain
Windows smashed in the night's deep scoop
Fat wobbles as you scream
Tin waves on tiled winds
Screaming bored
Screaming fear
Screaming like knife crime
Don't come round this way again
On the stairs, a pan of penne pasta and baked beans
stews in gelatinous globs
From the tarot deck, you pull the nine of swords.

Dream Lover

In the dream, you were packing to leave with your worst ex-boyfriend/The plan was: starting over in a trailer he'd converted from a squat red van, which in reality (by which I mean outside the dream, but you sort of know it in the dream as well) belongs to your husband/Oh there are lots of points in the dream when boyfriends and husbands and friends you slept with fade into and out of one another — when their bewildering sameness confuses you so extremely that the paternity of your baby becomes unclear/Or maybe there is no baby, yet/You are not sure if the dream takes place today, or at some past moment, or in a ceaseless liminal limbo, its possibilities fluid as the viscous dream texture/Your love shifted from dream man to dream man, as though the disparate emotional bonds of your life had let loose from time, unleashing havoc on the people who hurt you and even the one who did not/And why is the van parked in the long summer grasses by Slade Ravine?/Your ex-boyfriend is crying his hacking grief/You really do love your husband, you're telling him — it's important to tell him this, pathetic in his dressing gown and slippers/And there is another not-quite boyfriend to whom you've also told lies in the dream/In the dream he is very small/He is waiting at his dead mother's house to share the fact of your love with relatives, who say they've been worried/They're happy he's found you, after all that trouble with the last one/Still, he seems unimportant in the grander view of things/Though of course he'll have to be dealt with and his clamouring family will come to hate your guts/But back to what's vital: you have a baby now, you're telling him — the ex in the caravan — a baby with black hair and fatty legs and grey-blue eyes with golden streaks that glow when she's happy or the sun moves across them, like your own/like the sky.

After School Round Jackie's Nan's

1. Round here, breathe deep. Collapse in the fat brown armchair. Happy Shopper custard creams and thick, hot mugs of tea, poured from the old white ivy-patterned pot. Watched by matching cups and saucers they never use.

2. She needs say nothing on arrival — just offers her cheek for a whiskery peck. Waves of that scent: clean washing, cheap perfume, potpourri. Grange Hill and the breeze moving net curtains.

3. A chocolate bar if she fancies one. Or a ham sandwich on white bread. In the summer, strange salads with little cubes of cheese, pickled onions and sardines. Nan tells her, *Circle something nice in the Avon catalogue*; asks about her boyfriends (Jackie don't mention blowjobs behind the big bins).

4. Her schoolbooks, covered in bathroom wallpaper, scatter out from her bag. She's shrugged it off in the hallway, next to the shelf of Danielle Steels. The coat stand, where there's always that duck-handled umbrella.

The impossibility of impermanence
settles over these early evenings,
like a fog of peace.

Sket

After Dizzee Rascal

I'll forgive you, but you weren't on my side, damn!
Not ever — remember that day, on the train?
When the little girl with her face, so pretty,
hair in pigtails, turned right back
to stare at you, hands waving gentle, fast.
And her mother stepped forward as if to attack:
What you done to my little girl!
I said, *Not my man*, I said, *Not him, he ain't
done nothing wrong.* You were full of shame.
Hated me for loving you. Hated me, but
I couldn't understand why. Wracked my brain.
Wondered if this was really all just Daddy
Issues; your disdain, your mother closing the door to her house.
The way you said *slag* like it was my name. I got
no pleasure — cried tears like it was breaking my heart.
And here you are, *Sorry, I'm sorry I ruined
us.* Pleading at the other end of the phone all, *But,
but you know I never meant it.* Babe, you went
too far — I click the phone shut. I'm not going back.

Crazy

After Eminem

It was one of them wet, normal days, rain splashing
hard against pavement; crisp packets, pigeons fighting
for scraps of old crap. A toddler calling out, *Bye-bye*.
We stood on the beach, looking out at muddy river water.
Something came up to breathe and I thought of all our kisses,
and how they don't mean nothing now.
And how when things were new,
I took you home, said, *Dad,*
I met the one this time, as if we was characters in a play.
Now I lay my head on your shoulder. We're castles
in the dry sand.
And you'll admit (won't you?) you were well out of order,
so I can forgive you/forget about her.
But first, let me close my eyes, for just
a minute, and remember when we were brand new.

Yattie

After Jehst/Chester P/Kyza

You told your mates, *She's no Einstein.*
You said, *She loves my cock.*
You were stood under the galvanised steel piping
of some scaffolding, doused in evening light;
stood next to your parked car
with the slick coolness of a crime.
And it's true, I liked riding
you in the back of that car;
screaming while you did me from behind.
Tight minge, tight thighs.
But my mind
is not in my thighs.
My IQ's higher.
That's why I
wait for your brother behind
that dive bar — tell him: *Get them in,*
gin and tonic, nice and slim.

The Blues

I am not happy, I realise, as I pour milk into coffee the way I do: with one slop.
Coffee spatters over cup's rim and across clean tablecloth,
leaving a trail of flecks the colour of old blood.
I'm dabbing the flecks with a wet napkin and looking at the clock on the wall over my friend's shoulder when I think: this is unhappiness, what I'm feeling.

And all around there are other people at tables.
Conversation a steady drumroll beneath the clatter of glasses and crockery —
liquids being poured into vessels, wind blowing at the door.
It opens and closes again.
Tap   tap   tap.
The spoon makes circles in the coffee as I stir.
Not even sadness, this feeling I have,
it's enduring, like the long note held at the end of the last song.

And the air is too hot, and my neck feels sticky under my hair.
And on the street outside a little girl with dark skin and a winter coat lets go of her balloon, of course she does, her chubby hand gasping after the string of it. Eyes total Os following the balloon, which is drifting off into the endless sky,

the sea,

the belly of a marine creature.

All that blue.

Eastenders. A Classic. 2001

After Kate Durbin, who said, 'I wanted to reveal the script. You see, we are all carrying it.'

An Indian restaurant (orange walls, tingly music, Slater family meal in freefall). Mid-shot on Big Mo. Sound of a door slam. We hear Kat call: *Zoe! Come here!* Smash cut to outside. Wide shot. Darkness indicates late evening. The streets are empty. There's a sense of something ominous looming; there's the impression of cold. That tingly, ambient Indian music, like rising panic, carries from the last scene and fades into rushing air. Zoe's wearing a dark, lacy skin-tight dress with narrow straps, short; it's dotted with white and lilac flowers, there's a tiny pink satin bow at the front. Her long, mousy hair swings in the wind and with the force of forward motion. Kat is several paces behind her, cleavage exposed. She's in a red dress with black splotches and a black patent leather coat that flaps as she runs. Her black bob moves like a wig. Zoe shouts without turning round, *No! I'm fed up of you picking on me all the time!* Kat: *I'm not picking on ya!* It's one long tracking shot as Kat follows Zoe. They're storming ahead, curving in front of the flyover, round through the closed market. Flashes of blue and white striped tarpaulin. Abandoned stalls. Zoe, shouting, not looking back: *Embarrassing me in front of everyone!* Kat, imploring: *Just listen to me will ya?!* Zoe: *I'm going. There ain't nothing you can do about it!* Kat's arms move faster as she increases her pace, *Do you want a bet?* she screams. We can see part of a seafood truck in the background, the blue font across the white front. *Shellfish Bar*, it reads above the locked hatch; below the hatch, *Fresh Shellfish*. The wall behind is papered in posters. Kat trots faster still, trying to close the distance between their bodies: *We'll go and ask Dad together, shall we? See who he listens to!* Zoe: *Why don't you just leave me alone!* They pass the launderette. Kat: *Because you're not going to Spain.* Zoe's screaming over her before she's even finished, mouth wide as a yawn: *Yes, I am!* Kat grabs Zoe by the arm and spins her around so they're facing. We're close on Zoe's face. She has a thin silver necklace and, in her ears, a pair of silver or diamond studs. The back of Kat's head is in shot. Zoe: *Get away from me!* Close-up shot of Kat: *No!* They're outside the pub; an abundance of flowers blooms from the window boxes, dripping down in red and green waves over maroon walls. Close-up shot of Zoe, jaw clenched: *You don't rule my life!* Close-up shot of Kat, who's speaking levelly, as if to a child: *You're not going to Spain. And that's that.* Kat is in red lipstick; her long diamante earrings swing and shimmer. Close-up shot of Zoe: *Why not?* Close-up shot of Kat: *Because I said so alright?* Close-up shot of Zoe, she's not shouting, but still, she's furious: *And I have to do everything you say, do I?* Close-up shot of Kat: *No . . .* she gives the slightest tremor, some internal struggle as she hesitates at the threshold and then decides to carry on — but before she can continue, Zoe loses it. Close-up of Zoe.

Zoe, yelling, her voice hoarse with the graze of rage: *You can't tell me what to do! YOU AINT MY MOTHER!*

The camera pulls back to a wide shot of the women, with the street in view. The road runs back behind them, like the past. Zoe turns, charges away towards the square, leaving Kat behind. We notice Kat's bare legs.

Kat: *YES I AM!*

On the last word, cut to extreme close-up on Kat. Light from a streetlamp is falling across her face; you can see how her cheekbones have been illuminated with highlighter. Her expression sets and then falls. Extreme close-up on Zoe; she's utterly still. Extreme close-up on Kat. A stripe of fringe hangs down past her eye, resting on the side of her nose. The theme music plays: DUFF-DUFF/DOO-DOO-DOO . . .

A Sonnet for Jackie's Mother

On the estate, they called her a mad bitch,
(that fucking mad bitch)
because of her temper, and all that hair.
She grew herbs in her garden, like a witch,
and her stick-thin children looked fed on air.
She took amphetamines for the cleaning,
smoked weed every afternoon;
at fifteen, pregnant, she gave up dreaming,
smoked weed and cleaned and worshipped the full moon —

Told her children there was no one above them.
Oi, they better take that look off their face.
They stand in the yard blowing bubble gum,
she picks herbs, says the neighbour's a disgrace,
waves her secateurs at the open sky...
You know you're fucked if she catches your eye.

A Snapshot, 1983

Of course, on the nightstand, your rollers.
You'd placed them there in *almost* regimented rows.
Sat on the bed's edge, unfurling your custard-coloured hair.
Deft, arthritic fingers — the oval pearlescent nails;
maybe you didn't notice they were smudged.
It would have been very like you —
easing rollers from that thin hair.
Pride in a slapdash neatness.
Your aspirational glamour was the mid-century brown of the satin eiderdown,
lipstick in slightly the wrong shade, slipped onto your false teeth;
polyester shift dress, your jacket a copy of a copy of Chanel.
We loved your floral smell that clung to our clothes, perfumed our skin.
I see you turn back to us laughing on your way to bed,
securing your rollers with a bobby-pin.

Jackie Eats Out

She thought baked potatoes were the most depressing food.
They were.
No. She didn't care what you said about how fluffy white, ethereal,
peaks breaking into snow crystals,
overcooked, dripping, salt-smeared good they tasted.
You savoured the great leathery skins of them.
Soft, flavourless innards: drenched in butter or cheese or both.
She'd yet to understand it.
Their weight — that fist-sized bulk.
The black-death sense of living history that was the shape of a
baked potato on your plate.
And you didn't have to tell her that the potato would look
anachronistic in a Medieval drama.
Whatever.
She liked the present.
Its stillness.
The subtle umami of Japanese flavours,
like sushi, dipped in plum-coloured sauce.
And the umber-orange glow —
that most modern of things.
The span of an illuminated night sky.
Streaks of puce.
How only pollution creates that.
The deep chemical perfume of petrol
on fire.

Crevasse

At the cliff edge of motherhood, a waterfall sputters over rock's daggered face — Long moments in between surges of yellow pain — The nine of swords, again, bearing down their horizontal load — And the piercing strike of the next one, and the one after that — Down into the curdled abyss your familiar self tumbles — Her mouth shut against the hard air — Life's great surprise — Out of you steps a person, naked and screaming.

Eating In

Today, I read a poem about eating peaches after sex. The poet luxuriated in sticky sweetness; warm, fragrant juices, on her mouth and the sheets. I've never eaten peaches after sex, but once I sat naked at the foot of my boyfriend's bed, still fizzy from orgasm, and ate cold leftover curry with a spoon, straight from the takeaway tin. The container sent its metallic hum across my teeth. I upended the last of the yellow sauce into my throat as my boyfriend looked on, his face a grimace of horror and arousal. I licked my oily, spiced fingers and stepped into dirty knickers, laughing and sated.

Slag / noun:

She wants it all that slag
That dirty, dirty slag
Sloughed off and thick as treacle
She wants it more than you do
She'll get it too, probably
They do get it
These slags
Smelted
Legs open
Mouths wide open
You wait and see what she does with that wide open mouth
Sparks erupt from iron ore
Her black pleather mini skirts
Everything cavernous and bubbling and stinky
Everything soaking wet
So wet you could never dry it out
Never drink it up
That slag
Stretch marks pulled back like a threat
Sex played, like a game of roulette
In her leopard-print high heels
With her stretchmarks and all that pain
I think she's smiling
That bothers you, doesn't it?
And all her wanting.

I Imagine Looking at an Oil Painting, Which Doesn't Exist

A woman hangs, horizontally and face up, from an iron bar/She is suspended by meat hooks, piercing through her thighs — abdomen — chest/Her head thrown back/Anvil heavy and unsupported.

Her blonde bob is rendered with short, fast brushstrokes/The movement of hair on canvas/Streaking through the yellow colours so you can see how the artist has got there — the beiges and browns, the ochre/The background is a vast abstracted warehouse.

The painting has a fluid quality/Still, her body feels weighted/Like a rotten thing/Putrid/Bloated/About to explode.

Her face is contorted with yearning/Her skin is alabaster/Pink splotches on the fat parts/Blood bubbles thickly where the hooks pierce her skin.

I hope you find each other.

Subchorionic Hematoma

There, inside my steep walled womb,
an egg of blood.
The nurse moved the wand with precise turns.
I had lost dark clots, and concrete-coloured strings of meat —
held them in a wad of tissue and tried to identify human parts:
an arm the length of a fingernail;
some dot of foot.
My boyfriend clasped my hand — he was already crying.
The nurse rotated the wand inside me and said:
There's your baby.
She was no baby — she was a pulsing pearl,
wedged into a far nook of me.
And as the egg bled its bleed,
she pulsed her pearly pulse
and became my daughter.

Serving Officers

At the hill's tip, two boys sat by a portacabin.
Dark terror cylinders, like a psychopath's pupil,
dense with the intensity of a latent propulsive force,
swung easily as corpses over their shoulders,
threatening, yet totally indifferent to you —

You,
standing in those market-bought Mary Janes;
your bitter washing-powder scent on the ragged wind.
Sharp wind on bare legs, puckered like raw chicken skin.
Maybe the night before we'd danced in pubs —
this same boy
who slams the rifle's wooden heel
on the fleshy heel of his hand.
You'd felt his fingers, or his friend's fingers,
at your waist's skin.
Now, he shoves the rifle behind him;
inspects your picture on the plastic card with a dull glance,
nods to his mate in the portacabin, and the iron gate

                                                           swings

                                      open.

Chicken legs exposed, you serve soup to his commanding officer.
Serve this war the way you serve the next one
and the one after that: pulling your skirt down over your knees,
polishing silverware in the lamplight,
bending low with the ceremonial offerings of your people,
port and Madeira, blood-thick.
What is spilled by the officers, you wipe with a damp cloth.

Hot / adjective:

If you can't be good-looking — you might as well perform it
Show them all
You know what it means to possess hotness
Possess it like a tiger possesses hunks of gazelle
Devouring
With teeth like platinum credit cards
An online yoga class
Tone your arse, with gym membership
A Peleton —
Jewelry in gold vermeil
Stilettos or platform trainers
Get your thin, spiteful white-girl lips plumped up
They'll be kissable then
And suggest a prowess at blow jobs you do not possess
Who cares?
It's the performance that's important
Performing its importance
Blow dry your hair extensions with that $400 dryer
Those ombre waves cascade like a veil across the truth
Pull it back
Like you'll pull back his foreskin with your tongue.

A Thought on Valentine's Day

Remember that episode of Eastenders where Tanya buried Max alive in Epping Forest and then, almost immediately, drove back and dug him up — monologuing a litany of his misdeeds as he choked on lumps of dirt and sobbed into soiled shirtsleeves?

I've been thinking about that today.

I don't know why.

After Swimming

We stand by the river eating chips; wet hair whips our faces.
Knickerless.
In the wind, under the plastic flume —
twisting tubes of yellow/green where just now we whizzed
outside ourselves.

Salt burns paper cuts on our water-wrinkled fingers.
Vinegar and chlorine on our tongues and the air.
Cars speed by, flashing headlights in the glow of street-lamps;
orange on orange.

We suck vinegar off our fingers.
Suck the ends of our chlorinated hair that just now underwater
floated around us like soaking clouds while the hands of all these
boys ran over our wet bodies.
Up our legs.
Their lips our lips/For once I am not only watching.

You'd never call a 🥿 dog a shoe

Dove Wing

The sky in South London was white-grey,
dove wing colours,
leaking through my lover's blue curtains.

And later, there was a plum taste
on the tongue of this other boy — who loved me,
and tried to say it, but

everything changed before he could.
Possibility's smashedness.
You felt the whole world veer off course —

even though you were far away,
naked in your lover's single bed,
where New York was only an idea from movies.

His voice as you moved deliciously,
tangled together, like serpents,
like two halves from the same broken thing.

A plane has hit the Pentagon.
Glass, all shatters.
A million futures, all splintering.

Captions, written in blood.
We watch the towers fall.
The television flickers.

All day, we watch —
eat tea and biscuits.
Smoke cigarettes.

My lover cooks me vegetarian sausages
and frozen potato waffles with beans.
The spoon tastes like metal.

Breath from my mouth.
Dust billowing.

Those wide streets where I'll walk and walk —

I'll lean inside footprints,
to the Earth's black granite belly,
its gushing crystal water . . .

Oh.

You spend years
imagining lobbies —
looking out over chasms where they once stood.

Peering through wire fences.
Wire that some dove-wing grey
as the South London sky.

You close your eyes.
The click, click: court shoes on marble.
You dream about escalators;

elevators —
in your dreams everything rises up.
Or the wreckage . . .

Steel frames and dust all around.
Either way, you still panic.
And the boys I kissed.

Shot in the head.
Dead or ruined in the hot desert,
avenging this . . .

Thing.

This.

You lay in your lover's arms,
trembling at the enormity.
Shock visible on your skin,

like tiny ripples
on the skin of a river.
How water stretches where it meets the estuary

resisting,
before it becomes the sea.
And still that dove-wing sky

leaks in through the windows.
Time before the terrible future
becomes now.

The hot skin of your lover
peels away from your own hot skin.
Two separate things.

A plane has flown into The Pentagon.
The blue curtains move as you rush past them.
The television flickers.

Longing

In the tall blue fridge, there is a hunk of unwrapped cheese. A bloom has erupted on the surface, like a caution; like the calm before the mould sets in. I touch the white stuff. It is soft, like the fur on a petal, like the chickish down on his birthmark, which I stroked before I . . .

I was free then. I was searing rods branding thick days.

Now, a precise ice-cold blast of fridge air —

>Tragic kitchen scene.
>Mouth stuffed full of mouldy cheese.
>Outside it's winter.

Up the Common

My mother said no —
Not with those children
(or any children).
Those children, with their thick South London gobs.
And how we used to weave mazes through undergrowth;
bushes needling our skin.
Deep clean scent of earth on our knees,
elbows —
a den of newspapers.
Headlines none of us ever read.
Their red tops,
the yellowing pages.
Spidery letters —
fading girls with the best exam results,
prettiest faces.
Yellow flowers too,
tiny petals splayed neon stars.
Hot spheres of blue at the very centre.
And all around those children, who were us.
Edgeless, dangerous with possibility.
Our South London gobs were thick,
like the sky.

Hungry Eyes

You're a feast for the eyes, he says.
His pupils smack thick green lips,
hunting sweetness, drooling.
Buds of teeth sprout in smooth black gums;
gnawing at my fleshly cheeks —
that forked tongue dipping in a ketchup of blood.
Low growls of utter pleasure, not mine . . .
Ah! Whose delight is whose!? —
lost in the maul and pain of it
I'm consumed.

He Sees Me

In the karaoke bar — I'd finished an out of time, out of tune, rendition of the Beautiful South's 'Don't Marry Her' — he pulled my friend to one side — *Who is that?* He said — he was asking about me — he said, *She's incredible* — I heard it — I sashayed away — downed another gin and tonic — I saw how in his eyes my tight arse/blue eyes/shameless extroversion — a desire stew — an incredible revelation — I was the sun breaking into shafts of light — I was the taste of tequila after salt, and then the lime.

Fuck me.

A Haiku About Promiscuity

Bled on his blue bed.
The tall one with eyes like tar.
New one likes it rough.

Jackie Rides the Night Bus

At the back, on crisscross woolen seats, a delicate redhead in a satin kimono reaches into her silver rucksack and pulls out a McDonald's bag, wet with grease.

Jackie slips off her shoes; curls up on the seat like a prawn.

The woman eats the fries, holding each one in her mouth as though it were a straw, dipping her head precisely, like a shorebird, so that the chip is coated in ketchup from the little pot in her lap. Then she sucks it up, chewing gently, so gently, before she swallows.

Jackie feels a wave of nausea, like a warm breeze, the cinnamon flavour of Aftershock coating her mouth, stale music ringing in her ears.

There's a Black punk up front. He's very clean, for a punk. Leather collar covered in spikes, snakeskin Doc Martens, a sharp citrus smell and a green afro. Face full of piercings.

I want to lick him, Jackie thinks, noticing the jammy layer of grime on her own bare feet.

And the white guy with stains on his ripped t-shirt, BO and coarse matted hair across his chest, mumbles about corruption, tries to sell his poems to a drunk businessman, tells Jackie she looks as if she needs a good poke . . .

Of course, Jackie misses her stop. Wakes up at the bus garage with the driver shaking her arm; stumbles out onto the street as the sun breaks open another grey dawn.

Put Your Hands Around My Neck and Tell Me You Love Me

Like a knife pressed to a throat,
I hesitate at a terrible threshold.
My flesh, strange in your hands,
throbs true as a flame's hot centre.

I hesitate at a terrible threshold.
Your razor-blade smile, twisting.
I throb, true as a flame's hot centre.
I'm not sure, at first, if you see me.

Your twisted, razor-blade smile
refracted in my wine glass.
I'm not sure if you see me, at first.
Your gaze is slant as you laugh.

You are refracted in my wine glass.
Our friend is telling a bad joke.
Your gaze is slant as you laugh.
I feel your hand slide along my leg.

The friend tells his bad joke.
I laugh in shallow waves.
Your hand slides along my leg
with a steady, indifferent rhythm.

I laugh in shallow waves.
Your wedding ring gleams.
And that steady, indifferent rhythm
pushes flat against my longing.

Your wedding ring gleams.
My flesh, strange in your hands
pushing flat against my longing;
like a knife, pressed to a throat.

Bad Sex

The bus red flashes across sleek puddle water/We luxuriate in our voices/A synchrony of glottal stops over the crunch of car tyres/Sirens wailing/And the slow soprano of other people/We stop at this Lebanese place for chicken shawarmas/The watery lemon yoghurt leaks down my fingers/A white yellow rain/You pass me a napkin/Order a cardamom lassi so sweet you pour it down the drain after two sips/We watch it slip through fat bars/Your mum's found this weird mole on her neck, you say/But it's probably nothing/Still, you've been thinking lately about mortality, and how maybe you do want children, after all/I tell you my dad won't leave the house these days/Not since that thing with the ducks/Suck the yoghurt out the claw of my ring/Topaz, which I think passes for diamond/If you don't know the difference/(And most people don't)/When our phones ring we switch them to silent/Finish our shawarmas leaning against a decommissioned phone box/Share a cold can of coke/The graffiti on the wall opposite reads BAD SEX.

Out Loud

The rounds of my body
Stomach,
Eyes, mouth, pores, cervix
Open utterly
Screaming.

All My Fears Now Are for My Daughter: A Sestina

Death, that was the big one —
the eternal hiatus, waiting.
I stared down its cleft to oblivion,
terror at my throat like terrible vomit,
and the acid bubbling in the devil's pit
spat back.

The thing is, you are only half-aware as he rolls back.
You are not thinking about death or the way one
thing leads to another. The smell from his armpit
stains the air and the dreaded waiting
for him to say something rises. That terrible vomit.
It's not me he wants, you think, *it's oblivion*.

Then, *Sorry Mum,* as the thwack before oblivion
shatters all my futures. Time winding right back
to how just before you were I used to vomit
your fullness from my belly, darling one.
Long years; purple loneliness and all that waiting.
Then they plucked you from me, like a jewel from a pit.

Now he digs in the mud, shovels a deep pit
where he'll sling you to rest your final oblivion,
as I stand by the window, as usual, waiting.
No thoughts in your head now. No winding things back
to the point you could have said not this one,
I don't trust his gait; his stench makes me want to vomit.

In court, he stands over a bucket of vomit —
as though he might retch a not guilty from his stomach's pit.
On the stand, an American girlfriend says he was The One.
She shrugs an apology, stares off, bewildered, into oblivion.
She's wondering how she never noticed, yet at the back
of her mind, there was drumroll foreboding, frenzied waiting

for God knows what — all her life perpetual waiting.
Grieving mothers heaving, spattered grief-vomit.
This is what it means to love without going back

to an era when death seemed the blackest pit
from which, no escape, the final oblivion
turns out to be this one.

I stand in my living room playing back your videos. I'm waiting
for the big one. Love's pressure rises like vomit.
In my heart I dig a pit. Sleep there darling, fall into oblivion.

Ties

Here goes the sickening tug as I untangle myself from what I'm bound to/Desperation's drip-drip; your voice, syrup-clogged with blame/I rub my dry fingertips together and focus on the sandpaper sensation/This guttural writhing/A childhood flash/All subject to your whims/Countervailing manipulation with manipulation/My own acid way/Burn through the resistance/Brand this scorched earth.

Slip Up Number Five

It was a mistake.

He'll say this about you, later,
to his wife.
Maybe even to his buddies.
Himself.
A mistake.
It sits on the screen like a relief of truth.
You know it, even as he moves his tongue up inside you;
even as he insists that you keep the lights turned up.
He wants to see his mistake in the flesh —
even
the smell of old Chinese food,
wafting from the bin in the corner,
the heat moving against the walls.
Inside and out.
The world burning all around.

It was a mistake,

he says.

The way your bodies changed shape to fit.
You said, I get it;
as if allowing his skin to move against your skin was the betrayal,
and not the way the universe cracked the possibility of this moment open,
like the egg of a sea.

Jackie Visits a Launderette in New York

1.
When she was sixteen, her hair hung past her shoulders, a dreamy chestnut mane with copper streaks that glowed in the sun and invited unwanted caresses from her father's friend Paul.

2.
You'll have to cut this, he said, *When you're forty and old. Hair like this don't suit old women.* And he took a long drag on a Benson & Hedges and offered the open packet with one hand while he held her hair with the other, balancing his cigarette in the corner of his mouth.

3.
They smoked like that, side by side. He held her hair, weighing it in his palm, as though it were made of gold. As though maybe he could sell it for beer money.

4.
Tonight, her hair is heavy still, and it's summer, and her heavy chestnut hair is damp with sweat. And she's forty already and doesn't yet feel old. The vast machine drums turn her clothes over and over. Tall windows steamy and vibrating.

5.
Earlier, jaded from the day, she sorted her clothes into piles according to fabric and colour. And as she held a pair of silk knickers up, inspecting the gusset, a group of Chinese tourists wearing long beige trench coats came into the laundromat speaking loudly in Mandarin or maybe Cantonese and snapping pictures of the washing machines with giant old-fashioned cameras, as though this place was magically implausible — the machines with their massive drums, the sweet hot air from the dryers.

6.
Now, it's just Jackie and a young Puerto Rican woman who is reading King Lear as she waits for her washing to dry, her baby passed out in a broken pram. The static from the dryer is creamy and tense — the way a storm cloud is tense — immense with the possibility of release.

7.

The whole city moist with potential and here she is, folding clothes so fresh from the dryer they burn her hands, thinking about Dad's friend Paul. He's dead, now; left a suicide note speculating that fallout from nuclear war might be escaped in some parts of Spain.

8.

Her silk knickers have shrunk, and her favourite white t-shirt has turned grey. She lifts her long chestnut hair, twists it round her fist and lets it fall back wetly, stepping into the humid night with a hefty bag of clean clothes. Fuck you Paul, you muthafucker.

Entropy

My son eighteen now, my manicurist tells me. She's holding the brush from the jar of red nail polish, millimeters from my nail. *My daughter nineteen*, she says, *My daughter work in business*. She paints a stripe of the polish across my nail. In my pocket, there's a plastic elephant my toddler handed me on the way out the door; the same scarlet colour as my nails. Its smooth weight is there against my leg, like the warmth from her foot on my thigh as she sleeps.

Twenty years ago, I sat in this same chair; this same manicurist gluing tiny diamonds to my big, freshly painted, toe. The red she used then was called Tasmanian Devil. She was swollen with baby, sweating with the physical labour of tending my feet. She kept stopping to sip cold water. She flashed grainy pictures of her ultrasound; showing me the whorl of her foetus on the square of mobile screen. The mobile had little diamonds glued to it too.

In the mirror opposite my middle-aged, postpartum breasts sag; my whole fat ageing self. My hands look the same, at least from the bird's eye vantage; only the wedding ring, and the threat of crepening. The sag of my manicurist's face too, those tiny coarse hairs just growing back above her lip. And the clotted red polish on the rim of the bottle.

A Rhyming Haiku About Class

High class champagne glass
Middle class amass houses
Working class don't grass

Lifeblood

Blood/Chunks of what I thought were you, as you really curled into the very wall of me/Held fast — you wanted to be here, I hope you remember that, hope it catches/Spider's web on synapse/Diverts you from the worst thoughts; gets you through the days when nothing can get you through the days/And how I wanted you too, if it matters/Hands across the lump of you; so afraid as they strapped me to machines that your horse-hooved heartbeat would fall silent/When they cut me open, pulled you from me, legume from muck/The oh no/Your possibility/Your black curls; your sea coloured eyes/Each of your ten fingers.

Lived Experience

Smooth as cracks on a South London ceiling;
I roll over on a new body.
Again, again — what you thought you were —
rolling on, like a spliff in Gib's room,
in 2001, or whenever it was.
Fleshlier than these women, all bones.
Body is a flesh house.
Home feels clammy, like the other side of truth.
I bend it for my purposes;
return there when I need to.
The elemental rumble of community —
authentic spice.
They keep speaking down; my mumbles
rise up the tall thin streets in writhing echoes.

Dispossession

Light fell through the curtains in ribbons of gold;
you gave your weight to the cage of my bones.
The air billowed gently; pleasant and cold.

Sheets on the floor spread in rippling folds,
my breath rose wetly in quickening moans;
light fell through the curtains in ribbons of gold.

Summer heat surged, our secrets all told,
you whispered you loved me; our love was your home,
as the air billowed gently, pleasant and cold.

Impossible, then, we might ever grow old,
we lay as idle as sun warmed stones,
and light fell through the curtains in ribbons of gold.

You by my side and I became bold;
and the world felt safe, and sexy, and known.
The air billowed gently, pleasant and cold.

Oh, but
              you left
                            and I won't be consoled
I waited, years, for your call on my phone.
I remember the light and the ribbons of gold;
how the air billowed gently, pleasant and cold.

New Year's Couplet

Year of the Dragon, 1988

In the courtyard where Chrisp Street Market met the estate, low-rise government buildings, pimpled façades glowing white- grey; dirt in pavement cracks sprouted wiry new grass, spiky like chin whiskers. Market's call, *a pound a pound a bananas a pound,* rumbled under a strange piping rhythm and frenzied drums. My gummy hand clasped the buggy where my sister slept. This puppet dragon writhed with the legs of so many people, its mouth, manoeuvred by bamboo sticks, yawned paper flames. Human feet in ornamental slippers scuttered over concrete. Red and yellow pompoms dripped; red lanterns shuddered in the cold's steam. The great serpentine twist of a mouth, eyes were malevolent slits, crescent teeth gleamed cream moons. Not much later, you see, someone tiled that same dragon on the floor of the municipal swimming pool, where we learned to doggy paddle in neon armbands — mosaic blue-green tiles replaced with this ravenous carmine animal whose purpose was the consumption of slim little blonde girls. My banshee defence as this first fear set its electric alive through my body, veins a conductive circuit. I jolted in any direction, away from the terrifying water rippling shapes in contented dragon's breaths, as the dragon's static eye followed me up to the safe vantage of the viewing gallery.

> Behind glass, I sucked on Frazzles and sweet Ribena; senses heightened to the cloying syrup, tongue playing at the grazed skin on my thin purple lips — from this ruminative distance my blue eye met dragon's black eye and we nodded in mutual knowing.

Year of the Tiger, 2022

Our eyes met. We nodded in mutual
knowing. My mouth so dry; her black
hair so shocking — dark stripes across
nubs of yellow down, the colour of
chicks. In the commotion I whispered,
Sorry, and stroked her furry new cheek;
she bared claws, growling.

      Stuffed with tiger, I shuffled across Ladywell Fields; cumbersome blimp waiting for the hormone cocktail to kickstart what it must. I smelled of synthetic prostaglandin and natal blood; my hips ached. My long scarf dragged on the ground. Every now and then, surges compelled me to squat, rotating my pelvis, breathing: breathing. In the trees, wires from broken Christmas lights swung like vines. The grass was heavy with old rain. Dirty molten snow dripped from low hospital rooves; mud clung like terror to my white trainers. A little boy streamed down the gummy slide, squealing, *you can't catch me*. Days passed. My boyfriend rubbed the hot pain in my back. In my cell, I writhed on government lino, the whole air a sustained moan. I opened my throat and banshee wailed, vomited in another cardboard bowl; these stinking offerings discarded across the room as I rang and rang the red bell, retching. Still, the tiger slept inside me, her breaths, slow purring — utter contentment. You see, it's not always possible to override nature. I sat very still as the anesthetist plunged a long needle into my spine. Above my aching pelvis the surgeon cut a wide smile and set to work, yanking tiger cub; pearls of sweat glittered on his brow, like he was pulling roots from deep in the earth.

Pretty in Pink

In a locked cubicle, I watched, and two lines turned pink.
Time stretched its elastic and whole worlds burned pink

The sky curved out as I curved out too, a fertile expansion.
Tight against the ledge, all my burgeoning edges yearned pink

Life's long loneliness halved, cells expanded, body doubled.
In sour sweet amniotic juices, a not-yet person gurned pink

Hormones diluting meanness, I laughed my guileless laugh.
Dipping paintbrush in its pot, nursery walls adorned pink

On the news, a girl, abandoned to the November frost, died.
Her caterwaul drowned out; yet another family spurned pink

Sucking hot hospital air; retching, air hot as breathing hot fire;
I beg relief, then needles/slices/tugging, a baby emerged pink

The newness, at my age — say it — a new name: *Mother*.
Teaching: red, blue, green — see, my daughter learns pink.

About the QR Codes

The poems *Crazy*, *Sket*, and *Yattie* were written in response to rap tracks, using misogynistic insults from the tracks to explore romantic relationships.

Access the tracks by turning on your smartphone camera, or by opening a QR code reader app, then holding the viewfinder over the code until a link appears on your screen.

Crazy — "Bonnie and Clyde" by Eminem

Sket — "Jezebel" by Dizzee Rascal

Yattie — "The Trilogy" by Jehst

Previously Published

The poem 'Serving Officers' first appeared in *Mukoli: The Magazine for Peace*; 'The Blues' and 'Longing' were first published in *Harpy Hybrid Review*; 'Slip Up Number Five' first appeared in *Eunoia Review;* 'A Snapshot 1983' was first published in *Squawk Back*, 'All My Fears Now Are For My Daughter: A Sestina' was first published in *Ballast*.

With thanks to these publications for supporting my work.

Acknowledgments

With all my thanks to: Billy Beswick, CBC writers' group (particularly Amy and Jess), and to peers and tutors at The Poetry School. Special massive thanks to my man, Darren Xuereb — I'm yours.

Many of the poems in this collection were shown in an installation under the title 'Slaggy Connections' at the Theatre and Performance Research Association's annual conference at the University of Leeds in 2023, and as 'Being Slaggy' at Camden People's Theatre SPRINT Festival in 2024. I'm grateful to staff and audiences at both venues, and to Gerald Lidstone at Goldsmiths, for supporting that work.

With thanks to Matt and all at Red Ogre Review for the tireless work on this volume.

About the Author

Katie Beswick is an award-winning writer from South East London.

Her range of work spans scholarship, art criticism, theatre, music theory, poetry, prose fiction, and journalism. She is the author and editor of numerous books, features, and articles, including *Making Hip Hop Theatre: Beatbox and Elements*.

Her poetry has appeared in *The Lit*, *English: Journal of the English Association*, *Ink Sweat & Tears* and *Harpy Hybrid Review*, among others.

She works at Goldsmiths University of London.

About the Artist

Jamie Wheeler is an artist, designer, and theatre-maker from the United Kingdom.

Jamie designs and makes everything from theatre props and sets to accessories and drawings.

He also teaches acting and directs productions at several universities and drama schools.

About this Book

This book is published by Red Ogre Review and Liquid Raven Media under the fiscal sponsorship of Independent Arts & Media.

Red Ogre Review

https://ogre.red

Contact Red Ogre Review

info@ogre.red

Independent Arts & Media

https://artsandmedia.net